The Good Girl

By Anonymous

THE GOOD GIRL.

6

PUBLISHED BY JOHN METCALF,

WENDELL, MASS.

THE

GOOD GIRL.

—◦◦◦—

J. METCALF....WENDELL, MASS.

1832.

THE GOOD GIRL

The Good Girl always minds what Her father and mother say to her; and takes pains to learn whatever they are so kind as to teach her. She is never noisy nor troublesome; so they like to have her with them, and they like to talk to her, and to instruct her.

She has learned to read so well, and she is so good a girl, that her father has given her several new books, which she reads in by herself, whenever she likes; and she understands all that is in them.

She knows the meaning of a great many difficult words; and the names of a great many countries, cities, and towns, and she can find them upon a map. She can spell almost every little sentence that her father asks her to spell; and she can do a great many sums on a slate.

Whatever she does, she takes pains to do it well; and when she is doing one thing, she tries not to think of another.

If she has made a mistake, or done any thing wrong, she is sorry for it; and when she is told of a fault, she endeavours to avoid it another time. When she wants to know any thing, she asks her father, or her mother, to tell her; and she tries to understand, and to remember 008what they tell her; but if they do not think proper to answer her questions, she does not tease them, but says, "When I am older, they will perhaps instruct me;" and she thinks about something else.

She likes to sit by her mother, and sew, or knit. When she sews, she does not take long stitches, nor pucker her work; but does it very neatly, just as her mother tells her to do. And she always keeps her work very clean; for if her hands are dirty, she washes them before she begins her work: and when she has finished it, she folds it up, and puts it by very carefully, in her work-bag, or in a drawer. It is very seldom indeed that she loses her thread, or needles, or any thing she has to work with. She does not stick needles on her sleeve, nor put pins in her mouth; for she has been told these are silly, dangerous tricks; and she always pays attention to what is said to her.

She takes care of her own clothes, and folds them up very neatly. She knows exactly where she puts them; and, I believe, she could find them even in the dark. When she sees a hole in her stockings, or in her frock, or any of her clothes, she mends it, or asks her mother to have it mended; she does not wait till the hole is very large; for she remembers what her mother has told her, that "A stitch in time saves nine."

She does not like to waste any thing. She is unwilling to throw away or burn crumbs of bread, or peelings of fruit, or little bits of muslin, linen, or silk; for she has seen the chickens and the little birds picking up crumbs, and the pigs feeding upon the peelings of fruit; and she has seen the ragman go about gathering rags, which he sells to people to make paper of.

She is so dutiful and industrious, that her parents often take her with them to ride.

When she goes with her mother, into the kitchen, and the dairy, she takes notice of every thing she sees; but she does not meddle with any thing, without leave. She knows 013how puddings, tarts, butter, and bread, are made.

She can iron her own clothes; and she can make her own bed. She likes to feed the chickens, and the young turkeys, and to give them clean water to drink, and to wash themselves in; she likes to work in her little garden, to weed it, and to sow seeds, and plant roots in it: and she likes to do little jobs for her mother: she likes to be employed, and she likes to be useful.

If all little girls would be so attentive and industrious, how they would delight their parents and their kind friends! and they would be much happier themselves, than when they are obstinate, or idle, or ill humoured, and will not learn any thing properly, nor mind what is said to them.

PLEASURES OF WALKING IN THE FIELDS

I'll go to the field a for some flowers,
The fields are so lively and gay,
How sweet they are after the showers!
I could play in them all the long day.

Don't run from me, dear pretty lambs,
I never will hurt you, indeed;
You may play by the side of your dams
Or frisk it about in the mead.

Perhaps the sweet cowslip is here,
That hangs down its pale yellow
head,
The cuckoo-flower lovely and fair,
And the daisy encircled with red.

In the wood I shall find the blue bell,
And the pretty anemone too;
The meadow sweet down in the dell,
And the violet with beautiful 017hue.

The sweet-scented hawthorn I see,
And the roses that sweeten the
breeze;
But none of them sweeter to me
'Than the woodbine that twines
round the trees.

But who made these beautiful trees?
And who made these delicate flow-
ers?
Who sweetens with roses the breeze,
And refreshes the fields with his
showers?

'Twas my dear heavenly Father above
Who made every thing that I see;
And who, with compassion and love,
Regards a poor infant like me.

But what a sweet nosegay is here,
The best I will give to my mother,
And some to my school-fellows dear,
And some to my sister and brother.

Note from the Editor.

Odin's Library Classics strives to bring you unedited and unabridged works of classical literature. As such this is the complete and unabridged version of the original. The English language has evolved since the writing and some of the words appear in their original form, or at least the form most commonly used at the time. This is done to protect the original intent of the author. If at any time you are unsure of the meaning of the original meaning of a word, please do your research on that word. It is important to preserve the history of the English language.

Taylor Anderson

Printed in Great Britain
by Amazon

75727140R00020